JN411155

Non-matter

Non-matter

A collection of new poems by Lee Hyun-ho
Translated by Agnel Joseph

아시아

Contents

NON-MATTER

POET

Part 1

The Invention of Love

The people who invented optical devices must've
been in love, don't you think?
The desire to see every tiny little detail of their
love must've led to the microscope
The desire to stop time when they were together
must've led to the camera
The desire to reveal the secret of the celestial body
that was their love and shine far and wide must've
led to the telescope
so that not even a single gesture, a single look
slipped by unnoticed
and a moment was remembered for eternity
Blindly we wanted to go together to the farthest
future we could go to

A world visible only through the lens that is my love

A world that is not worth even a grain of sand compared to my love gets sucked into a black hole

like a convex lens that focuses sunlight on a point and causes it to ignite

even if that fire turns everything into ash

Love must've invented optical devices, for one person

If Love Really Exists

It’s what I love
It’s a name I call sparingly
When it looks back
we believe we’re in love

We discard it at times
At times it leaves us
In a moment like this
anything could happen
that turns us into each other’s demons

It’s what we loved
A name that memory will love
We love, we loved, we will love

Without it, there's no love

Without it, there's no love

If someone asks me about love

I'll answer: It is love

Then you nod as if you understand

With a look that says you know it well

As if it really exists

We stand outside the bracket

and toss it into the bracket

Angel of the Future

There were strawberries in the fridge Don't know
where they came from They were red and fresh
I was hungry I think I liked strawberries

When I came to my senses only a pile of green
hulls remained on the plate
I worried about things that needed worrying
Who could it be? That red and fresh heart with
black seeds stuck all over

If I respectfully offered the plate with only the
hulls left on it to someone
and said, These are actually strawberries
would we be able to start new strawberries

Strawberries are originally like this Green fruits with nothing that's edible
If someone scratches their head like they've realized it only just now
does that mean we've given birth to new strawberries

I put the plate with the hulls neatly spread out on it
in the fridge that always maintains its temperature
The strawberries bereft of their flesh will stay fresh longer, won't they

Leaving the ripped green here

why is that I feel this way

Revelation

The cat's movements look just like brushstrokes
When the cat moves stealthily, it's the brush moving carefully
When the cat zooms around frenetically, it's the brush dashing off in a single stroke
As if invisible hands are using the cat as the tip of a brush
to write something in the room

Like letters written in the air with fingers
Like footsteps on a sandy beach where the waves return

The cat crouched in a corner of the room looks

like a period
Like the eyes drawn at the end after the painting
is done
The cat as it grooms itself with great care
looks like a brush being cleaned
Like how ink spreads in the water bowl where the
brush is washed

As the room is colored in silence
a voice rubs against my ankles

The only thing human in this room
is the cat
I feel like I should meow

Guess I should come to my senses now
while crying like a cat asking to be fed

I think I should wash a cup of rice

Things That Become Clear At Last

Two shadows seemed to shake
It happened in a dream I can't remember well

I strolled till late and slept early
I felt like I had left somebody behind in my dream

I hadn't slept such a dark sleep in a long while

Did I not dream
Or did I dream a black world

I thought as I rubbed my damp eyes
It felt like somebody had spilled me out of my

dream

Time to wake up, let's open the window

The night didn't seem to be over yet

I couldn't see how many shadows were there in the darkness

The Wild

I cried even in my dreams
When I woke I was so famished
I could've made a meal out of my tears

Sadness is like a wild boar that descends on a home
Like a potato field it digs up with its tusks
Like corn stalks it uproots and crushes
To lay waste, to turn into ruin

Let's have courage and eat well
We're in a dream, picking a few unharmed potatoes from the trampled field
raising fallen corn stalks

weeping tears like grains of wheat

The hungry boar calls on the home again
The god that will rescue us from our dreams
seems to be wandering in a dream of their own making

I come across the wild boar and it stamps its hind legs
bristles its coarse hairs and fumes
With no time to even think of avoiding it, I freeze
My ribs are shattered by the sadness that comes charging at me

Tonight too I'll dream through my tears
Days like this will always be there
Because both we and the wild boar will always be hungry

Look, here comes sadness

Midsummer's Divine Office

The mosquito and I are close friends. Only the two of us are there in my room. My earth, my moon. I can't hate someone who rides my turbid breath and hovers around me like a satellite. It'd be nice if it came like a sled dog running through a blizzard, but it doesn't have a tongue to hang out and bite and run with. I lift up my pj's a little more. I lie as if nailed down, undress, and look up at the buzzing ceiling. Someone among the mosquito's distant ancestors must've drunk the blood of Jesus. The mosquito must be a distant relative of the Son of God. I somehow feel at peace. I run to sleep like someone riding a dog sled. When I open my eyes,

there will be a dark red spot on the palm of my

hand, a crumpled wing, and a rice-grain-sized nothing, and I'll scratch my swollen flesh until the day this universe ends.

Improvement

A sheep's wool continues to grow

The sheep we know today
come from the pairing
over a long stretch of time
of only sheep with good wool growth

A sheep's wool grows like it's breathing

The grass the sheep graze on becomes wool
The relentless wool blocks their eyes
covers their legs
and finally presses down on their bodies

A sheep's wool grows endlessly

A crashing cumulus
the sheep sinks down helplessly
unable to withstand the weight of its own wool
A bundle of wool that can't move itself

Even now the sheep's wool grows

A sheep that evades the shears
dies slowly
Somebody left
after making me who can't leave you

A sheep's fur . . . grows

A sheep
lying in a field of decapitated grasses
bleats
choking under the weight of its cries

Midwinter's Divine Office

If I meet with an accident in the snow I'll cover myself with a thick layer of snow I'm that sort of a person Today too I lay wrapped in my blanket all day long Packed in the blanket I return to myself My body warms the blanket and the blanket warms my body and even God can't scoop me out of this self-generating universe If I pull up the blanket to my forehead this darkness becomes my sky From head to toe I'm that sort of a person I'm not ashamed even if my innermost warmth is found out by the blanket Is this love? If I meet the night in the snow I'll brazenly build a snow mountain on my naked body My body heat will melt the snow and I'll lie trembling in the snowmelt as more snow falls on me thick and dense

An Evening of Eating Peach Worms

A black-headed worm was wriggling
when I looked after taking a bite out of a peach

"They say if you eat a peach worm you become a beauty."

The milky-faced person smiled
and turned off the light

and we turned into beauties

In a room where only the sound of peaches being eaten could be heard
it felt like someone in a different world somewhere

was biting into a dinner
full of the scent of peaches

Everyone was beautiful in the dark

Open Ending

The novel I just finished reading
ends with the protagonist walking into a snow-covered cedar forest
When I closed the book and looked up
endless rows of cedar trees were lined up in front of me
The forest looked like it would never
never ever end

I had started living in a closed room at one point of time
so this was inside somewhere
Inside a dream or inside my imagination or inside a novel or if not that
everything must be inside a certain life

And it snowed

It snows

I felt like I had to keep on walking
as if it had already been decided
Hoping my premonition was wrong I
stood still for a moment with my eyes closed
while it snowed
If this was not a book that God had read long ago
If someone opened the door like opening a book

It was snowing
Cedar trees like deep footprints

Non-matter

If it's a non-matter
that can be sliced through like air with your fingertips
that doesn't hurt even if half of it is torn off like dough
because it really has a soul

I'd pull out about half of the soul and send it flying like a thunderbolt
with the unbearable urge to become matter
that a person who knocks on a window with pebbles all night long has

The soul stuck in one corner of your room is a

non-matter

and so you unwittingly overlook its inside

and every time you do that the soul grows ruddier bit by bit

and the lights now come down and sit at a slightly higher place

and the night grows a little brighter for some reason

On a night like that, the look in your eyes when they land on me inadvertently

—with the power of that vivid non-matter

a soul that's like an apple that someone took a bite out of and tossed

bears fruit that look exactly like hearts
and the moonlight shadows of ten fingers
are placed like a giant wing on a back that's sleeping sideways

Now the world doesn't need any poetry
A soul is a soul, an angel an angel
Dreams of matter and the flesh of non-matter
fill the empty space in the world that God took a bite out of and chucked

On such a dawn the soul finishes praying
There's a prayer to finish souls
There'd be nothing surprising about it

if you open the window and see an angel flying
away

Because there really are souls

Part 2

Action

The trees on the street outside the window are being trees on the street
Since when have those trees been standing there just like trees and waving their leaves?
There's no sign of the birds that have flown off trying to be birds
Until when will the café glass windows reveal their insides?
Chairs rest on the floor on all fours vacantly
On top of them, hearts beat and keep beating as hearts
The door doesn't stop opening and closing because it's a door
The leisure of this afternoon is peaceful

so people sip coffee that's going cold and
everybody's doing well
Evening arrives to be evening
without even saying, Excuse me
And because I'm me
I'm afraid to move my chin that's resting on my
hands at an angle

A Children's Playground with Swings

Two children ride a swing They each hug a metal chain and sit in the small seat with their backs to each other They sync their side-crawls and squeal Looks like they already know that the most they can do is sway with their backs touching and laugh On another swing a child lies bent over with his belly resting on the seat He keeps unbending his knees and stretches his two hands in the air Looks like he wants to fly Like he already wants to get away from the ground A child on yet another swing spins in one direction Look like it's fun when the badly entangled chain unravels in a whirl Where did I learn the phrase, Life flashes by? I sit on an empty swing My stretched legs look like arrows that're missing arrowheads I feel hungry in no time at the playground In the neighborhood I used to live in when I was young the labyrinthine streets were our playground Looks like the meals I skipped back then have returned Looks like hunger is pushing hunger's back on a swing that's swaying by itself

Sunday

Kids from the kindergarten wake me in the morning. In the night, silence and cicadas were crying in turns. Now outside the window the alley cat that ran away from me last night and the old man who was sleeping in the pavilion with his belly exposed are nowhere to be seen. The children disappear into the yellow kindergarten.

Life feels like a colony of death.

I eat while watching a wildlife documentary. The eagle lives only by letting go of the sky it enjoys. It snatches prey from the lowest altitude of its life and returns to the sky. The rabbit's eyes shine between the eagle's claws as if they'll explode like a supernova.

And yet the earth spins.

Tonight too the old man sleeps in the pavilion with his belly bared and talks in his sleep. The alley cat slinks past him. Silence and cicada cries turn on and off. Tomorrow, bright yellow children will awaken my closed eyes. I, a safe haven, have stayed here far too long.

Like a spell, I nod my head.

Irreversible

"I think a bright shirt will look good on you."
And so
I took the plunge and bought a new shirt

But I splattered soup on it And
no matter what the stain won't go away
Now I can neither wear the shirt nor throw it away

Standing in front of the mirror, despite myself
I see myself
wearing only a shirt that was bright

You, the first and last person who connected me
and bright colors and shirts

The last of the first, the first of the last

"No one makes stains intentionally."

And yet

the inevitable happens inevitably

As if laundering your heart

as if you've scrubbed it out

you wear a heart that's like a new dress

I try boiling the shirt

but the irreversible stain remains

And so

And yet

Eyes are Mirrors of the Heart

Within them
live hearts that graze on sorrow
long-antlered hearts that drink tears
A few hearts peek outside and kick with their hind legs
Under the sky where misery floats
snorting puffs of warm breath
they grind their antlers

When the wet season starts with abandon at the mere touch of somebody's fingertips
a herd of hearts crosses a transparent fence
creating a waterway
The heart with the longest antlers knows—
sadness is a kite that flies higher the farther it goes

away

tears are a reservoir that gets endlessly torn down and rebuilt

When the misery that feeds the hearts blows a long whistle again

the hearts that've shed their horns without realizing it

retrace their nomadic path that has become brighter

scratch their itchy antlers on their eyeballs

and cross the fence that's grown a little thicker

and chew quietly like a cloud

on sprouting sadness and surging tears—the contributions of that misery

When I see on the path where tears have licked my face
the footprints of high-heeled hearts
the rattling of fallen antlers and
somebody who's crying while rubbing their eyes with the back of their hand
hearts that grow antlers step inside and sit down

There's an antlered heart
that looks into my eyes reflected in the mirror
on nights when broken from the long dry season
they hurt to live again

Cliché

The rain that falls at the moment of parting
feels like a cheesy movie
Even bad actors will look
sad enough in such rain
They'll look sad, enough

Raindrops nip a face that's turning away
On the road, on the roof, on the glass window
The rain laughs while smashing expressions

When will it rain?
When it wants to

Even a person completely soaked

has some place left to get wet in the rain, I guess
They're always in the rain like fools
It's like a TV drama I've seen a hundred times

Unable to bear their own weight
the raindrops let go of themselves
and the person looks like they'll rust away in the rain
You end up watching till the end
even as you swear, It's the worst!

When will it stop raining?
When you close your eyes

Hello

I played with a friend in my dream. From morning to night,
we shared trivial days that anyone would quickly forget. We ate, walked, sat and rested, and
cried. We kept crying tears that didn't make us breathless because we were in a dream
"Are you happy there?"
"No."
It was a friend who went into the water by himself many years ago and didn't come out
The dead friend wasn't a ghost
but was simply a friend who was dead forever
Even in our dreams we knew
that it was not everything

Hero

Things that are at a standstill complete the entry ban. I stop and keep still like a recon soldier who has discovered a mine. I maintain order in the world. A car that drives up the no-entry road passes by me and disappears behind the corner. Children come pouring out of a kindergarten by the no-entry road. A stroller steps on the no-entry sign that has an X in the middle of an arrow. But I prove this place is off limits by standing still. Like I'll be in that position even a thousand years later. Bird calls resonate from the trees on the road like a warning sound. Dark clouds pass over roofs at the end of the road. I'm banned right now. The moment I enter, the world will collapse. I bear a debt to the world. While you cross the entry ban

Two Hearts

There was one heart There was another heart together with that heart

Though they were hearts

one heart made it possible for the other heart to be One heart was beside the other heart

Though they were only hearts

one heart lived because of the other heart Both hearts beat as one

Though they were merely hearts

there were two hearts that covered the night and lit a candle

Though they're said to be hearts

when one heart left, the other heart turned into a weed fallow When one heart disappeared the other heart became a broken vessel

Though they're only hearts

there was a time when we in our hearts were our hearts

Though they're hearts

Where Have You Been At Night?

I mistake a sofa abandoned in the alley for somebody bent over crying and am startled. It's not a false vision but a false feeling. A notion that somebody's there, a feeling that somebody was there. But the sofa isn't an abandoned person. It's something like a place in life where you can't sit again, like the horoscope for November seen in December. Things that'll disappear just as they secretly appeared.

"Even a mouse hole has sunny days." The daily horoscope pops up on the smartphone at midnight. This is what a night walk that repeats daily is like. Fate changes masks in the minute between 11:59

a.m. and 12:00 p.m., and you hang around in front of the front door in anticipation of that unfamiliar fate. Hoping there'll be nobody bent over crying on the other side of the door.

Darkness is like furniture. The darkness inside the house is now like a sofa that has been broken in to fit my body. I fumble for the light switch for the daily horoscope. Even though I know it well, when I turn on the light I look around the house for no reason. A light like artificial leather covers the mouse hole. As clear as you who're not in front of me

It’s not a true vision but a true feeling
Something like the smell of heart
that can only be touched with closed eyes

Night Eating Syndrome (夜食症)

The bird died so I threw the birdcage away
The fish died so I threw the fishbowl away
I don't think I can raise them again

I throw my heart away
Something that used to live there has died

An unbearable dawn

At the place where I dumped the birdcage and fishbowl
I find a chipped rice bowl
that somebody has thrown out after wrapping neatly in newspaper

I squeeze rice into the rice bowl to the brim
and eat the dead bird and fish

With my outermost face

Ending Credit

A stone that somebody has throne
flows away like a ripple created in the reservoir of night

I can't tell when I have to wake up
I feel like I have to watch over those names to the end

As if everything will disappear like bubbles when I turn around
Not forgetting is truly like a movie

As soon as a staff appears from the emergency exit and starts cleaning
I rise hurriedly like I've been waiting

Like someone's who's been caught out

Feeling like I'm surfacing after a deep dive
Leaving behind a screen I've never seen the end of
like a sunken ship

An Eternal Walk

Let's walk together a bit more
You said that once
so we're

still walking
Those sweet words

I couldn't tell how much 'together a bit more' was
Was 'a bit more' time or distance Was 'together' temperature or feeling
How much longer did we have to be together for it to be a bit more

As for the words 'let's walk,' I couldn't help but

walk

Slowly, so that walking didn't turn into running
But without going too far

Until sweet words call
me you thy thou us
like a blackout

POET'S NOTES

When I meet a beautiful sentence,

I might be able to write it differently, but in the end I feel like that's the only way I could've written it.

A sentence that can't be touched anymore. A living organism of a sentence in which not a single word can be added, removed, or changed. A sentence in which the words fit perfectly. A sentence that will collapse like a house of cards if one letter is changed. A sentence that's like a taut rubber band. A sentence whose life is cut off just by adding or removing a punctuation. A sentence in which every word is erected like the pillar of a bridge. A sentence that maintains its rhythm like a series of stepping-stones and stumbles if a stone is moved even a little. Beautiful sentences in which not one thing can be fiddled with.

Beautiful sentences are beautiful because there's

nothing that can be done to them. Beautiful things are like that. I know it doesn't make sense, but if you can't do anything about deficiency and ugliness then it's beautiful. Having written this far, I recite that everything was inevitable. The inside of me is full of traces of things I lost, things I let slip, things that passed by me. There is also a back view of you who never looks back again. I was always helpless in front of them. I couldn't help the me who was helpless. I was at my wit's end.

I can't do anything about the future I'll face even as I'm unable to deal with everything right now, either.

POET'S ESSAY

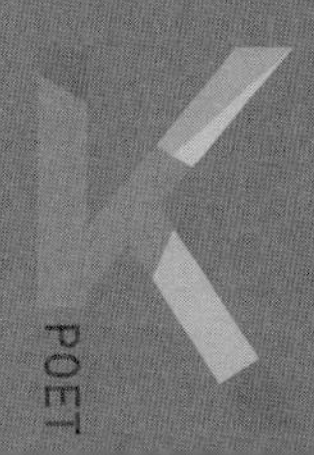

The blue whale is the largest and heaviest animal on Earth. They grow to about 24 to 33 meters long on average, with the largest specimen discovered measuring up to 33.58 meters in length and 190 tons in weight. An apartment floor is usually around 2.5 to 3 meters high, so this basically means that a ten-story apartment building is swimming in the sea. I count the floors of the apartment I see outside my window one at a time and am surprised again. I can't believe a creature of that humongous size lives on this planet with me.

If the blue whale is the largest and heaviest animal on Earth, then the photo titled "Pale Blue Dot" is the most famous space photo in history. It's a photo of Earth taken by Nasa's Solar System space probe Voyager 1 from six billion kilometers away in space on February 14, 1990. A dot that's so small you can't find it unless you look closely, according to American astronomer Carl Sagan Earth viewed from far away in space looks like "a mote of dust suspended in a sunbeam."

Just as this vast Earth that I can't cover even if I were to walk all my life is just a mote of dust when seen from space, the blue whale is also a tiny existence compared to the sea it lives in. Things that are small while big and big while small. When I think of the blue whale and the pale blue dot, I feel like they resemble memories. A memory that pops up in a huge world of unconsciousness, which in the words of psychiatrist Carl Gustav Jung is "everything of which I know, but of which I am not at the moment thinking; everything of which I was once conscious but have now forgotten."

Earth is a "pale blue dot" but all humanity lives and has lived there. Everything they've experienced and will experience is there on that dot. Some memories are like that for me. In the sea of unconsciousness, everything I've seen, heard, and felt in my life may be asleep, but the place where my life stands is a piece of memory that abruptly comes to mind anytime. It's a face in that memory, a moment's expression that flits by on that face. Like a tugboat dragging a stranded ship, one memory on the verge of sinking leads me. You in my memory are my pale blue dot.

Whales cannot live without surfacing occasionally to breathe. Like a whale swimming in the deep sea that sometimes rises to the surface to breathe, some memories also come back to life. The memory is alive, so even if I try to forget it, it seems to rise from the deep sea of oblivion to survive. Maybe it's doing this not to survive but to save me. You're a whale or the blowholes on the middle of its back in my subconscious. The scene of the whale breathing on the surface and spouting water through its blowholes is beautiful to look at no matter when.

Today I happened to think of you while looking at a picture of a whale. There are promises that've been kept and some that haven't been yet. Hello, friend. In our memories I'm pale and you're blue.

COMMENTARY

The Pronunciation of Love

Park Dong-eok(critic)

One person misses another person and writes a poem. This simple fact that constitutes Lee Hyun-ho's poetry creates a special structure for his poems. His poetry doesn't appear to address the reader directly. Instead, the poet's words seem to be directed first to somebody he loved. He talks to somebody far away, at times while being overcome with emotion, or at others, only after becoming quiet enough for his sadness to subside. And we're simply eavesdropping on his voice. In that case, what we're looking at is the back of the poet. What's revealed in this collection of poems is not the poet's face but his back that's more genuine.

Also, what we need to strain our ears for in his

poetry is something like the appearance from the back of his words, the earnestness audible in the quiver at the end of his words. For example, he says he wants to forever remember every little trace of you, every little moment he spent with you. He lays his heart bare and says that he's suffocating under the weight of his tears after you left, that he's collapsing every night under the weight of the sorrow that comes rushing toward him. What leaves a deep impression with these belated confessions are his counter-questions that reassess his heart. Can a heart that has lost its flesh, like a strawberry with only the hull at the top left, grow back again? Can I continue to be me like the evening that's just an evening every day?

Somebody may confirm the presence of a person left behind in these sad counter-questions and ask skeptical questions about love. Can love be more than just saying I love you? One's heart belongs to oneself and words are only words. Even if somebody confesses their love, they don't know if it carries the same meaning, the same texture, the same time for the other person. Lee is well aware that in the end the word love cannot overlap two hearts. The word love is always lacking. Love doesn't get conveyed through a confession of love.

But on the contrary aren't we pronouncing love in new ways every morning because of that gap? Lee does that. With a certain hesitation and melancholy, his tongue pushes the word love out from his mouth. He repeats the pronunciation of love with effort. In his poetry we see how he fills the gaps when words fall out of place. We learn from him the way of translating objects like cameras and telescopes into positions of looking at a loved one. Even when we turn toward each other, we learn the mindset of saying I love you. Instead of throwing around the word "love," we learn the technique of changing into "it." Instead of writing "I'm with you," somewhere out there in another world somebody learns to depict a dinner scene filled with the scent of peaches.

Love is not something to be dug up and dissected. Lee's poetry carefully wraps up love and grips it. Cherishes it. Perhaps more genuine than the authenticity of love is the warmth that remains in your hand after your love is over. Perhaps what we call soul is that posture where our backs are still facing our love even in the moment when we can no longer meet them. Perhaps the hungry heart that wishes to reach there even as it exists here may be the meaning of non-matter or metaphysics. At least in Lee's poems, the words "soul" and "heart" are used as a knot that connects two people. In this collection of poems, these two words are always connected to two hearts even when referring to one person.

A person who sees the world through his or her lover's heart even when alone—what is the significance of that gaze? To borrow a philosophical observation, Alain Badiou who considered love, revolution, and poetry to be the same said that none of them are given but are inevitably encountered. In short, love is not something that can be meaningful in a give-and-take relationship. Just as revolution is an event that hasn't yet arrived, two people in love don't know what love is. They simply tremble with anxiety as they face love together. They jointly hold the word "love" no matter what happening love may bring about. Two tongues advance together toward the common revolution of love.

Likewise, Lee emphasizes the ontological anxiety that love causes. And that anxiety can shift to an event that renews the ego through an encounter with one's love. He repeatedly talks about two people facing each other. About the eyes of your love whom you looked at with your back to the world. About the fact that you can't break away from the reflection of yourself in your love's eyes. In the end, even when you love, even after love, you're inside your love's eyes. Like this he dreams of love even as he's heading to a predetermined sad ending, like gladly having an accident in the snow. So the love he pronounces instills patience and courage in us. It allows us to have daring and generosity. Thus the more we pronounce the word "love" in this poetry collection, the more we realize that it is a way to transform our existence by taking love as a trial. He walks alone into the snow that falls like a stain, like sadness, like a nightmare.

But even at that moment, your love should be your only lamp. He or she can no longer be your lover, but there are moments when the world becomes a little brighter just by recalling the words he or she loved, believing in them, and pronouncing them again. Even if it is a faded memory, there are moments when you can rely on it and love the world. If you have to store something in the heart of a person that has been left behind like a chipped bowl, it must be your love. And so, this collection of poems depicts the back of somebody who can't easily turn around and leave the theater while the end credits are playing. In the end, they stand with their love, resolving to walk a little longer with them. That way, through their love, they gauge the time, distance, temperature, and feelings they have to endure in the future. They rely on their love and walk with the world.

WHAT THEY SAY ABOUT LEE HYUN-HO

"The story told by Lee Hyun-ho's poetry makes us imagine a story that might not have existed if something had not existed in the first place or if someone had existed in a different way. Perhaps, the absence of the here and now can only be sensed through an image of the unknown that exists only insignificantly, like dust. That's why in Lee's poetry certain regrets and certain prospects form a single narrative through a single image. Something like a so-called flash of light, appearing, then quickly disappears but leaving a special afterimage, is stored as images in Lee's poems. And, paradoxically, because these images are so trivial and weak they're subordinate to certain stories that won't disappear after existing only momentarily."

— Kim Nayoung, "Thinking about the Fate of a Writer: On Lee Hyun-ho's Lend Me a Lighter," Munhakdongne Fall 2014

“The confusing statements and destruction of grammar that Lee makes full use of in various ways in his poetry contain traces of his efforts to express the complex and subtle workings of the heart in an impressive manner. He writes and erases countless times and sometimes even violates grammatical rules to reveal the state of a sensitive heart that can’t be fully expressed in words that don’t contradict existing language and grammar. Paradoxically, to break grammar one has to be proficient in it. From the prolix sentences Lee uses skillfully in his poems we can surmise that he’s a poet who has wrestled with sentences for a long time.

“He devotes himself to exploring a language that transcends the boundaries of language to express subtle changes in emotions and an endlessly expanding imaginary world without suppressing his romantic inclinations. Love is the ultimate ideal of his romantic passion and the fundamental force that drives his life. [...] What he wants to meet at the end of love is himself. His poems are somewhat different from the spirit of negation against society and institutions that are deeply entrenched in the tradition of Korean romantic poetry. Or perhaps, he is continuing a lonely fight to preserve human values as we pass through the peak of machine civilization that suppresses individual lives with a greater invisible force than before."

— Lee Hye-won, "Romantic Scenes of Dazzling Misfortune: On Lee Hyun-ho's The Name of Beautiful People is Alone," Siin Dongne June 2019

K-POET
Non-matter

Written by Lee Hyun-ho
Translated by Agnel Joseph
Published by ASIA Publishers
Address 445, Hoedong-gil, Paju-si, Gyeonggi-do, Korea
Tel (8231).955.7958
Fax (8231).955.7956
Email bookasia@hanmail.net
Homepage Address www.bookasia.org

ISBN 979-11-5662-317-5 (set) 979-11-5662-584-1 (04810)
First published in Korea by ASIA Publishers 2021

This book is published with the support of the Literature Translation Institute of Korea (LTI Korea).

바이링궐 에디션 한국 대표 소설

한국문학의 가장 중요하고 첨예한 문제의식을 가진 작가들의 대표작을 주제별로 선정!
하버드 한국학 연구원 및 세계 각국의 한국문학 전문 번역진이 참여한 번역 시리즈!
미국 하버드대학교와 컬럼비아대학교 동아시아학과, 캐나다 브리티시컬럼비아대학교 아시아학과 등 해외 대학에서 교재로 채택!

바이링궐 에디션 한국 대표 소설 set 1

분단 Division

01 병신과 머저리-**이청준** The Wounded-**Yi Cheong-jun**
02 어둠의 혼-**김원일** Soul of Darkness-**Kim Won-il**
03 순이삼촌-**현기영** Sun-i Samch'on-**Hyun Ki-young**
04 엄마의 말뚝 1-**박완서** Mother's Stake I-**Park Wan-suh**
05 유형의 땅-**조정래** The Land of the Banished-**Jo Jung-rae**

산업화 Industrialization

06 무진기행-**김승옥** Record of a Journey to Mujin-**Kim Seung-ok**
07 삼포 가는 길-**황석영** The Road to Sampo-**Hwang Sok-yong**
08 아홉 켤레의 구두로 남은 사내-**윤흥길** The Man Who Was Left as Nine Pairs of Shoes-**Yun Heung-gil**
09 돌아온 우리의 친구-**신상웅** Our Friend's Homecoming-**Shin Sang-ung**
10 원미동 시인-**양귀자** The Poet of Wŏnmi-dong-**Yang Kwi-ja**

여성 Women

11 중국인 거리-**오정희** Chinatown-**Oh Jung-hee**
12 풍금이 있던 자리-**신경숙** The Place Where the Harmonium Was-**Shin Kyung-sook**
13 하나코는 없다-**최윤** The Last of Hanak'o-**Ch'oe Yun**
14 인간에 대한 예의-**공지영** Human Decency-**Gong Ji-young**
15 빈처-**은희경** Poor Man's Wife-**Eun Hee-kyung**

바이링궐 에디션 한국 대표 소설 set 2

자유 Liberty

16 필론의 돼지-**이문열** Pilon's Pig-**Yi Mun-yol**
17 슬로우 불릿-**이대환** Slow Bullet-**Lee Dae-hwan**
18 직선과 독가스-**임철우** Straight Lines and Poison Gas-**Lim Chul-woo**
19 깃발-**홍희담** The Flag-**Hong Hee-dam**
20 새벽 출정-**방현석** Off to Battle at Dawn-**Bang Hyeon-seok**

사랑과 연애 Love and Love Affairs

21 별을 사랑하는 마음으로-**윤후명** With the Love for the Stars-**Yun Hu-myong**
22 목련공원-**이승우** Magnolia Park-**Lee Seung-u**
23 칼에 찔린 자국-**김인숙** Stab-**Kim In-suk**
24 회복하는 인간-**한강** Convalescence-**Han Kang**
25 트렁크-**정이현** In the Trunk-**Jeong Yi-hyun**

남과 북 South and North

26 판문점-**이호철** Panmunjom-**Yi Ho-chol**
27 수난 이대-**하근찬** The Suffering of Two Generations-**Ha Geun-chan**
28 분지-**남정현** Land of Excrement-**Nam Jung-hyun**
29 봄 실상사-**정도상** Spring at Silsangsa Temple-**Jeong Do-sang**
30 은행나무 사랑-**김하기** Gingko Love-**Kim Ha-kee**

바이링궐 에디션 한국 대표 소설 set 3

서울 Seoul

31 눈사람 속의 검은 항아리-**김소진** The Dark Jar within the Snowman-**Kim So-jin**
32 오후, 가로지르다-**하성란** Traversing Afternoon-**Ha Seong-nan**
33 나는 봉천동에 산다-**조경란** I Live in Bongcheon-dong-**Jo Kyung-ran**
34 그렇습니까? 기린입니다-**박민규** Is That So? I'm A Giraffe-**Park Min-gyu**
35 성탄특선-**김애란** Christmas Specials-**Kim Ae-ran**

전통 Tradition

36 무자년의 가을 사흘-**서정인** Three Days of Autumn, 1948-**Su Jung-in**
37 유자소전-**이문구** A Brief Biography of Yuja-**Yi Mun-gu**
38 향기로운 우물 이야기-**박범신** The Fragrant Well-**Park Bum-shin**
39 월행-**송기원** A Journey under the Moonlight-**Song Ki-won**
40 협죽도 그늘 아래-**성석제** In the Shade of the Oleander-**Song Sok-ze**

아방가르드 Avant-garde

41 아겔다마-**박상륭** Akeldama-**Park Sang-ryoong**
42 내 영혼의 우물-**최인석** A Well in My Soul-**Choi In-seok**
43 당신에 대해서-**이인성** On You-**Yi In-seong**
44 회색 時-**배수아** Time In Gray-**Bae Su-ah**
45 브라운 부인-**정영문** Mrs. Brown-**Jung Young-moon**

바이링궐 에디션 한국 대표 소설 set 4

디아스포라 Diaspora

46 속옷-**김남일** Underwear-**Kim Nam-il**
47 상하이에 두고 온 사람들-**공선옥** People I Left in Shanghai-**Gong Sun-ok**
48 모두에게 복된 새해-**김연수** Happy New Year to Everyone-**Kim Yeon-su**
49 코끼리-**김재영** The Elephant-**Kim Jae-young**
50 먼지별-**이경** Dust Star-**Lee Kyung**

가족 Family

51 혜자의 눈꽃-**천승세** Hye-ja's Snow-Flowers-**Chun Seung-sei**
52 아베의 가족-**전상국** Ahbe's Family-**Jeon Sang-guk**
53 문 앞에서-**이동하** Outside the Door-**Lee Dong-ha**
54 그리고, 축제-**이혜경** And Then the Festival-**Lee Hye-kyung**
55 봄밤-**권여선** Spring Night-**Kwon Yeo-sun**

유머 Humor

56 오늘의 운세-**한창훈** Today's Fortune-**Han Chang-hoon**
57 새-**전성태** Bird-**Jeon Sung-tae**
58 밀수록 다시 가까워지는-**이기호** So Far, and Yet So Near-**Lee Ki-ho**
59 유리방패-**김중혁** The Glass Shield-**Kim Jung-hyuk**
60 전당포를 찾아서-**김종광** The Pawnshop Chase-**Kim Chong-kwang**

바이링궐 에디션 한국 대표 소설 set 5

관계 Relationship

61 도둑견습 – **김주영** Robbery Training-**Kim Joo-young**
62 사랑하라, 희망 없이 – **윤영수** Love, Hopelessly-**Yun Young-su**
63 봄날 오후, 과부 셋 – **정지아** Spring Afternoon, Three Widows-**Jeong Ji-a**
64 유턴 지점에 보물지도를 묻다 - **윤성희** Burying a Treasure Map at the U-turn-**Yoon Sung-hee**
65 쁘이거나 쯔이거나 - **백가흠** Puy, Thuy, Whatever-**Paik Ga-huim**

일상의 발견 Discovering Everyday Life

66 나는 음식이다 – **오수연** I Am Food-**Oh Soo-yeon**
67 트럭 – **강영숙** Truck-**Kang Young-sook**
68 통조림 공장 - **편혜영** The Canning Factory-**Pyun Hye-young**
69 꽃 – **부희령** Flowers-**Pu Hee-ryoung**
70 피의일요일 – **윤이형** BloodySunday-**Yun I-hyeong**

금기와 욕망 Taboo and Desire

71 북소리 - **송영** Drumbeat-**Song Yong**
72 발칸의 장미를 내게 주었네 - **정미경** He Gave Me Roses of the Balkans-**Jung Mi-kyung**
73 아무도 돌아오지 않는 밤 - **김숨** The Night Nobody Returns Home-**Kim Soom**
74 젓가락여자 - **천운영** Chopstick Woman-**Cheon Un-yeong**
75 아직 일어나지 않은 일 - **김미월** What Has Yet to Happen-**Kim Mi-wol**

바이링궐 에디션 한국 대표 소설 set 6

운명 Fate

76 언니를 놓치다 - **이경자** Losing a Sister-**Lee Kyung-ja**
77 아들 - **윤정모** Father and Son-**Yoon Jung-mo**
78 명두 - **구효서** Relics-**Ku Hyo-seo**
79 모독 - **조세희** Insult-**Cho Se-hui**
80 화요일의 강 - **손홍규** Tuesday River-**Son Hong-gyu**

미의 사제들 Aesthetic Priests

81 고수 - **이외수** Grand Master-**Lee Oisoo**
82 말을 찾아서 - **이순원** Looking for a Horse-**Lee Soon-won**
83 상춘곡 - **윤대녕** Song of Everlasting Spring-**Youn Dae-nyeong**
84 삭매와 자미 - **김별아** Sakmae and Jami-**Kim Byeol-ah**
85 저만치 혼자서 - **김훈** Alone Over There-**Kim Hoon**

식민지의 벌거벗은 자들 The Naked in the Colony

86 감자 - **김동인** Potatoes-**Kim Tong-in**
87 운수 좋은 날 - **현진건** A Lucky Day-**Hyŏn Chin'gŏn**
88 탈출기 - **최서해** Escape-**Ch'oe So-hae**
89 과도기 - **한설야** Transition-**Han Seol-ya**
90 지하촌 - **강경애** The Underground Village-**Kang Kyŏng-ae**

바이링궐 에디션 한국 대표 소설 set 7

백치가 된 식민지 지식인 Colonial Intellectuals Turned "Idiots"

91 날개 - **이상** Wings-**Yi Sang**
92 김 강사와 T 교수 - **유진오** Lecturer Kim and Professor T-**Chin-O Yu**
93 소설가 구보씨의 일일 - **박태원** A Day in the Life of Kubo the Novelist-**Pak Taewon**
94 비 오는 길 - **최명익** Walking in the Rain-**Ch'oe Myŏngik**
95 빛 속에 - **김사량** Into the Light-**Kim Sa-ryang**

한국의 잃어버린 얼굴 Traditional Korea's Lost Faces

96 봄·봄 – **김유정** Spring, Spring–**Kim Yu-jeong**
97 벙어리 삼룡이 – **나도향** Samnyong the Mute–**Na Tohyang**
98 달밤 – **이태준** An Idiot's Delight–**Yi T'ae-jun**
99 사랑손님과 어머니 – **주요섭** Mama and the Boarder–**Chu Yo-sup**
100 갯마을 – **오영수** Seaside Village–**Oh Yeongsu**

해방 전후(前後) Before and After Liberation

101 소망 – **채만식** Juvesenility–**Ch'ae Man-Sik**
102 두 파산 – **염상섭** Two Bankruptcies–**Yom Sang-Seop**
103 풀잎 – **이효석** Leaves of Grass–**Lee Hyo-seok**
104 맥 – **김남천** Barley–**Kim Namch'on**
105 꺼삐딴 리 – **전광용** Kapitan Ri–**Chŏn Kwangyong**

전후(戰後) Korea After the Korean War

106 소나기 – **황순원** The Cloudburst–**Hwang Sun-Won**
107 등신불 – **김동리** Tŭngsin-bul–**Kim Tong-ni**
108 요한 시집 – **장용학** The Poetry of John–**Chang Yong-hak**
109 비 오는 날 – **손창섭** Rainy Days–**Son Chang-sop**
110 오발탄 – **이범선** A Stray Bullet–**Lee Beomseon**

K-픽션 한국 젊은 소설

최근에 발표된 단편소설 중 가장 우수하고 흥미로운 작품을 엄선하여 출간하는 〈K-픽션〉은 한국문학의 생생한 현장을 국내외 독자들과 실시간으로 공유하고자 기획되었습니다. 원작의 재미와 품격을 최대한 살린 〈K-픽션〉 시리즈는 매 계절마다 새로운 작품을 선보입니다.

001 버핏과의 저녁 식사-**박민규** Dinner with Buffett-**Park Min-gyu**
002 아르판-**박형서** Arpan-**Park hyoung su**
003 애드벌룬-**손보미** Hot Air Balloon-**Son Bo-mi**
004 나의 클린트 이스트우드-**오한기** My Clint Eastwood-**Oh Han-ki**
005 이베리아의 전갈-**최민우** Dishonored-**Choi Min-woo**
006 양의 미래-**황정은** Kong's Garden-**Hwang Jung-eun**
007 대니-**윤이형** Danny-**Yun I-hyeong**
008 퇴근-**천명관** Homecoming-**Cheon Myeong-kwan**
009 옥화-**금희** Ok-hwa-**Geum Hee**
010 시차-**백수린** Time Difference-**Baik Sou linne**
011 올드 맨 리버-**이장욱** Old Man River-**Lee Jang-wook**
012 권순찬과 착한 사람들-**이기호** Kwon Sun-chan and Nice People-**Lee Ki-ho**
013 알바생 자르기-**장강명** Fired-**Chang Kangmyoung**
014 어디로 가고 싶으신가요-**김애란** Where Would You Like To Go?-**Kim Ae-ran**
015 세상에서 가장 비싼 소설-**김민정** The World's Most Expensive Novel-**Kim Min-jung**
016 체스의 모든 것-**김금희** Everything About Chess-**Kim Keum-hee**
017 할로윈-**정한아** Halloween-**Chung Han-ah**
018 그 여름-**최은영** The Summer-**Choi Eunyoung**
019 어느 피씨주의자의 종생기-**구병모** The Story of P.C.-**Gu Byeong-mo**
020 모르는 영역-**권여선** An Unknown Realm-**Kwon Yeo-sun**
021 4월의 눈-**손원평** April Snow-**Sohn Won-pyung**
022 서우-**강화길** Seo-u-**Kang Hwa-gil**
023 가출-**조남주** Run Away-**Cho Nam-joo**
024 연애의 감정학-**백영옥** How to Break Up Like a Winner-**Baek Young-ok**
025 창모-**우다영** Chang-mo-**Woo Da-young**
026 검은 방-**정지아** The Black Room-**Jeong Ji-a**
027 도쿄의 마야-**장류진** Maya in Tokyo-**Jang Ryu-jin**
028 홀리데이 홈-**편혜영** Holiday Home-**Pyun Hye-young**
029 해피 투게더-**서장원** Happy Together-**Seo Jang-won**
030 골드러시-**서수진** Gold Rush-**Seo Su-jin**
031 당신이 보고 싶어하는 세상-**장강명** The World You Want to See-**Chang Kang-Myoung**